MAURI KUNNA

THE BEST SPORTS BOOK
IN THE WHOLE WIDE WORLD

Translated from the Finnish by Tim Steffa

Crown Publishers, Inc.   *New York*

Excitement is high at the Dog Dell Stadium where many athletic events are under way. The steeplechase, the discus throw, and the women's high jump and broad jump are going on now, and athletes are warming up for other events.

A discus thrower

Warm-up exercises

A jumper

Water jump

Go Dog Dell

A shot-putter

Marker

An interview

Presentation of awards

Scoreboard and scorekeepers

Wind gauge

Broad jumper

3

Photo-finish camera

It looks like number 173.

Grrowf! Now that's the way to launch a javelin.

Track-and-field star Mick Might signs an autograph for Poochie.

The hurdlers are neck and neck at the finish line, with the exception of one who has decided to go *through* and not *over* the hurdles. The others break the tape at almost the same time. Who is the winner? It is the runner who first touches the tape with his body. This calls for help from the photo-finish camera.

Sniff's cleats are caught in his training suit.

The next event is a relay race. The Pawburg team is the favorite. "On your marks . . . get set . . ." orders the starter.

The starting gun is fired and the baton-carriers a[re] off like rockets.

The Pawburg team is in the lead.

But Betsy Bowser has forgotten to pass the baton, and Linda Lunge has grabbed Betsy's ear by mistake.

The Pawburg team must be disqualified. How embarrassing! And Betsy's ear does not feel very good, either.

It's time for the sprints, but Sparky is not up to running. Everyone is puzzled until Doctor Tonic locates the trouble—a tight running shoe.

Shot-putter Hannah Hunk has dropped her hanky, and an admirer rushes to retrieve it.

Annabel Anvil primps before her turn to go on.

Poochie hopes Ms. Anvil will have time to sign an autograph once her nails have dried.

Triple-jumper Shirley Shank concentrates hard and then jumps.

Whoops! One jump too many.

Race walkers must always have one foot touching the ground. Swing those hips!

Paul Vaulter is afraid of heights. He always takes along a parachute.

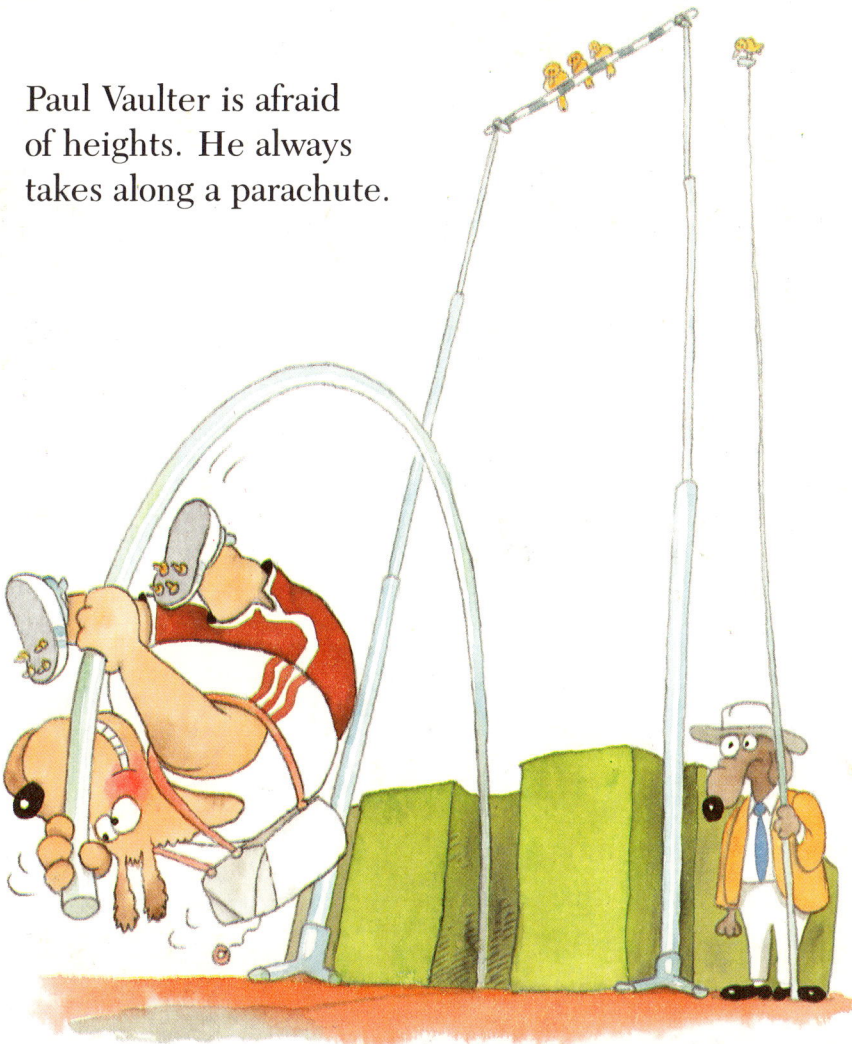

A high jumper "flops" over the bar.

Another jumper is suddenly stricken with a fear of flying.

The 10,000-meter (6.2 miles) run is the most grueling track event.

Fritz is a mouse with grit. His legs are too short for a long-distance runner, but now he is on his final lap.

Hooray, Fritz!

The Dog Dell Marathon is a popular sporting event. Hundreds of runners from around the world have come to participate, even weekend joggers.

The streets have been closed to traffic, and volunteers provide refreshing drinks along the route.

A lady out for a Sunday stroll had completely forgotten that a marathon was being run today.

Grandpa Goofus is being interviewed. He is the oldest runner, and he believes in taking along a lot to eat.

The marathon race got its name from the village of Marathon in Greece. According to legend, in 490 B.C. a Greek messenger ran across the plain of Marathon to Athens with the news of the Persian defeat. That trip was said to have been 42,195 meters (26.2 miles) long, and so that became the length of the modern marathon race.

This man is an armchair athlete.

TV mobile broadcast truck

Fans cheer the runners.

CHEAP POP

POLICE

Even the Dog Dell TV station is covering the run. Several mobile broadcast trucks are parked along the route, and a helicopter is following the runners.

Some athletes compete to break records, others to keep fit. Lance Lope wants to lose weight, and so every day after work he goes for a run, rain or shine.

Orienteering is another event in the Dog Dell Olympics. It involves the use of a compass and map to find check-points in a forest.

Some competitions are held at night, so a night competitor can't be afraid of the dark.

Yip takes a break in the blueberry patch.

Of course after a jog and a shower,
Lance rewards himself with a piece of cake.

Meanwhile a moose
eats the checkpoint.

13

Barney Buffoon gets
a high score for
his somersault dive.

9 10 10½ 9

Springboard

Backstroke

Butterfly

Riv

There's an important race going on in Dog Dell's swimming hall. It is the medley relay, and the teams are already warming up in their lanes.

The breaststroke, butterfly, crawl, and backstroke are the different swimming styles.

The freestyle is an event in which the swimmer is free to choose a swimming style. Usually it is the crawl because that's the fastest.

Poochie prefers the dog paddle.

Between events the Lotuses perform a water ballet.

ses the frog kick.

Crawl

A favorite rowing event is the eight-oar race,
but this one seems to have gotten off to a bad start.

Station judge's boat

Coxless pair and kayak

16

The coxswain steers the boat
and calls the rate of the strokes
to the oarsmen.

Canadian canoe

There's a motorboat race in Dog Dell Bay, and hydroplanes
are streaking around the course. One of them almost
overturns Salty's sailboat.

There are three waterskiing events: slalom, trick skiing, and jumping.

Diving can be an exciting hobby, especially if there's treasure to be found.

Each boat in a sailing race competes in its own class. Which class a boat belongs to depends on the boat's size.

FD
K89

These young ladies cool off by windsurfing.

The boats in offshore races are bigger and the courses longer. The longest voyage is around the world.
But sailing can be risky!

Show-jumper McMutt displays style even in difficult circumstances. But style doesn't determine points; a show-jumping competition is decided by the faultless clearing of the obstacles and the time taken to complete the course.

The obstacles are made of wood, but although they look sturdy, their upper parts are made to fall down if touched by a horse's hoofs.

A stable girl

The Dog Dell Derby is a popular event in which races are run for prize money. And there is competition among the ladies in the grandstand to see who has the most fashionable hat.

Horses are transported in fancy horse trailers.

Pitching horseshoes is not an equestrian sport.

Dressage involves three main types of pace: the walk, the trot, and the canter. But this horse also knows the steps to the fox-trot. What sort of points will the judges award for that?

Trusty Gallop takes the lead in a neck-and-neck race.

A rodeo rider on a bucking bronco

Harness-racing horses pull light, two-wheeled
carriages called "sulkies" and run at a trot or pace.

Polo players swinging their mallets

Whoops! There goes an autograph!

Gambling is part of harness racing.

Between races there is a great deal of activity as people place bets on their favorite horses or collect their winnings.

WC

TOTO

23

Main bunch

In road racing the faster riders suddenly try to break clear of the bunch.

Below, cyclists compete in a tandem race in the Dog Dell Sports Arena. These bikes have no brakes.

Tandem-cyclist Pat Pedal isn't getting much help from his partner!

Billy Bonk was well in the lead until he blew a tire and had to change it.

Carl Coot would like to compete, but he is afraid of losing his load of fresh eggs.

A sidecar rider tries to keep the bike balanced on curves.

Motorcycles go fast.
Drivers wear crash helmets, leather clothing, and thick boots and gloves for protection.

Motocross is a cross-country motorcycle race with steep climbs, sudden bumps, potholes, and mud.

Trail events are real balancing acts. Riders try to drive over rocks and logs from one point to another without letting their feet touch the ground. The winner is not necessarily the fastest rider, but the one with the least penalty points.

Speedway bikes have no brakes, so riders must pivot their bikes around corners. Their steel-soled boots come in handy for these power-slides.

Crunch drives in demolition derbies.

Pop Clutch is a go-carter.

Susie Slick prefers ice racing.

Here's a snappy dragster. Dragsters are driven in acceleration races over quarter-mile courses.

THE SNAIL

Formula racing is a dangerous sport, but Chico, the lead driver, has steady nerves.

Formula One cars are run at several races during the year. The driver with the most wins is named World Champion.

The Formula One is the fastest type of car. Auto manufacturers compete to see who can build the speediest model.

Here on the Le Mutts circuit, engines roar as cars circle the track.

The winner is already nearing the finish line, but where is Chico?

Nip and Tuck are taking part in a jungle rally, but they have lost their way.

When a blue flag is waved, a driver must let an approaching car pass. A yellow flag means danger and a red one, interruption of the race. A black-and-white checkered flag is waved when the winner crosses the finish line.

Chico should have won, but someone forgot to refill his gas tank at the last pit stop.

29

Target shooting has been popular for hundreds of years.

Archery is a great sport because persons of any age may participate.

The modern tournament bow is very different from the bow Robin Hood would have used. The modern bow has stabilizers and sights, and archers now use leather arm and finger guards.

Air rifles and air pistols are fired at a target 10 meters (33 feet) away. A telescope is used to check the results.

Above, Bruno shoots a pistol at a revolving silhouette target on a 25-meter (82.5 feet) range. This gun makes a lot of noise, so Bruno wears mufflers to protect his ears.

The range for small-bore rifles is 50 meters (165 feet) and for others 300 meters (990 feet). There are three shooting positions: prone, kneeling, and standing.

Bullets thud into a high "stop" behind the targets on the rifle range.

All marksmen know that guns, even unloaded ones, must never be pointed at any living creature.

Shooters wear specially designed leather jackets that do not restrict their aim.

Wild-boar shooters may use telescopic sights.

Lock and Stock use shotguns to shoot clay pigeons on a skeet shooting range. Lock shoots first at one and then another, trying to blast them to bits.

Barrel, the cat, prefers a slingshot.

Bert jumps over the pommel horse.

Betty executes a split on the balance beam.

Gymnastic exercise makes the muscles strong and supple and can be fun to do as well.

Ordinary gymnastic exercises can be done at home, but apparatus gymnastics is more difficult and requires a good coach and a big gym.

Rings

Horizontal bar

Mouse Y-scale

Pug on the parallel bars

Nelly performs on the uneven parallel bars.

Vic misses a vault.

Leapfrog

Hoop

Ribbon exercises

The Dog Dell Women Gymnasts rehearse their routine, accompanied by music.

Jill thinks the music is just too fast.

Bridge position

Poochie's somersault

Headstand

Bull wants to wrestle in the
featherweight class,
but he's too heavy so he's reducing
by jogging.

Bull is tired out from jogging.

Women's mud wrestling

Wrestling is one of the world's oldest
sports. Wrestlers are classified according to
their weight, and each one tries to pin his
or her opponent and win points for various
aggressive and defensive moves. In Greco-
Roman wrestling, opponents may not grasp
each other below the beltline.

Foil

Epée and sabre

34

"No grease allowed," says an official.

Referee

Fencing is an old form of dual combat. There are three types of fencing weapons: the épée and the sabre for men, and the foil for men and women.

The foil and épée are used to score "hits" on an opponent; the sabre also scores "cuts."

The foil and épée have electric leads on their tips. A wire runs up the blade, up the fencer's sleeve, and under his jacket to a signal light. When a hit is scored, the light comes on.

On-guard position

All fencers wear masks, gloves, and protective clothing.

The language of fencing is French. The president orders the fencers into the "on-guard" stance: *"Prets?"* (Ready?) And when everything is set: *"Allez!"* (Begin!). *"Halte, halte!"* (Stop, stop!) he yells. "Something is wrong. Hits must be scored on the torso."

35

Judo is a method of defending oneself or fighting without weapons.
A *judoka*, or contestant in a judo match, shows respect for the
area and the mat by bowing.

The Dog Dell Judo Hall, or *dojo*, is kept neat and clean. The *judokas* remove
their slippers before stepping on the judo mat, or *tatami*, to begin a lesson.

Karate is a method of self-defense developed
in Japan in which a person strikes
sensitive areas on an opponent's body
with the hands, elbows, knees, or feet.

Buster uses his
karate skill to chop
logs, since he has
broken his saw.

The purpose of judo is to throw an opponent so off balance that he is easy to tip over.

A *judoka* honors his opponent, and each training session begins and ends with a bow.

The color of a *judoka*'s belt indicates his or her degree of skill. A beginner's belt is white. Then comes yellow, orange, green, blue, brown, and the highest degree, black.

Karate involves concentration and self-discipline. It requires years of practice to master.

Sumo wrestling is an age-old Japanese sport. Sumo wrestlers are chosen at age twelve because of their potential to become men of great height and weight.

Punching bag

In the gym, other boxers practice with punching bags, weights, dumbbells, and by jumping rope.

Boxing is an ancient sport in which contestants fight with their fists. Boxers wear heavily padded mittens known as boxing gloves, and fight in a roped-off area called a boxing ring. Matches are fought in timed segments called rounds, and a round is over when the bell rings.

In the sparring ring a boxer tries to hit target mitts worn by his trainer.

Weights

Dumbbells

Jumping rope

Shadowboxing

If one of the contestants receives a wallop that sends him sprawling to the canvas, the referee counts the seconds and ends the bout if that boxer doesn't get up within ten seconds.

Referee

Heavyweight champ Ted Terrier signs an autograph.

A timekeeper, doctor, and judges sit at the officials' desk.

39

Dog Dell's weight lifters gather at the gym to practice. There are three types of lifts: the bench press, the squat, and the dead lift.

Brutus attempts a bench press.

In the squat, weights held across the shoulders are lifted from a deep knee bend.

Samson is a body-builder.
He thinks big muscles are very good-looking.

These body-builders are competing in the Mr. Muscle Contest.

In the dead lift, the barbell must be raised far enough so that the lifter's legs are straight.

A lifter's back is supported by a wide belt.

Official weight lifting involves three different lifts. In the clean and jerk, weights are lifted to the chest and then above the head. The snatch is a single movement of the weights from the floor into a braced overhead position. In the clean and press, weights are lifted to the shoulders and pushed straight up.

41

Cross-country skiing is a rigorous sport. In the Dog Slope Games, men and women compete in separate races. Skiers start out at half-minute intervals and each is timed individually.

Waxing skis so they slide smoothly is a difficult and important job. Leif, the head ski-waxer, has all sorts of gear, including a heat lamp and various waxes.

Annie *was* in the lead, but now she is getting tired and Sally is catching up.

Slick and Crusty are having problems because their skiis weren't waxed by Leif. Slick's skis are too slippery.

And Crusty's skis stick to the snow too much.

Sarge yells,
"Yield the track!"

The biathlon combines skiing and shooting. There are four shooting stops on the 20-kilometer (12 mile) course. The skier who finishes the course with the best time is the winner.

Frosty likes skiing long distances best and has just finished skiing 50 kilometers (30 miles) in the severe cold. Now for some hot juice.

FINISH

Snowmobile

This mouse has had it. His watergun is frozen solid.

Inaccurate marksmanship means penalty laps.

The skier must stop and shoot five times at each target.

After the exertion of skiing, it is difficult to hit the target. Each time a skier misses, two minutes are added to his total time.

Buster doesn't need snow. He has roller skis.

45

Ski jumping demands courage and control, and ace ski jumper Frank Flight exhibits both.

Jumpers are awarded points for the length of the jump and for style.

Frank will get plenty of points for this jump.

Judges' tower

Jumping is impossible on a windy day, but it is calm today.

Being a spectator here is cold, hungry work!

A freestyle, or "hot-dogging," competition is an artistic event involving ballet, hill stunting, somersaults, and turns off a ramp.

A trusty first-aid crew is always on duty.

This bird wants to compete, too.

This cameraman is filming the wrong person!

47

A four-man bobsled team consists of a driver, two middle men, and a brakeman. Every sledder must wear a helmet and goggles for protection.

And they're off!

Whoops! There goes the brakeman!

Poochie and Tyke love sledding.

This is a luge, which is driven lying down to reduce wind resistance.
The luge course is shorter than the bobsled course, but the curves are sharper.

A bobsledding race is one of the most dangerous of all winter events.

The sleds whisk down icy courses and around the turns at more than 90 miles (144 km) per hour.

These two mothers hope their sons will practice at home by sweeping the floors.

Curling is a game played on ice in which two teams of four players each compete in sliding curling stones toward a mark in the center of a circle.

Curling stone

49

This is a downhill-skiing course called the slalom. The skier must try to ski the slope as quickly as possible while steering through a series of flags known as gates. The gates test the ability of the skier to turn quickly and well. The skier with the fastest time is the winner.

Chair lift

ZORRO 10

CAMERA Niki

WoolaPoola

FI

Oops! Teddy didn't make it.

Snow gun

A snow tractor is used to smooth the ski run, and a snow gun to make more snow if the slope needs it.

The giant slalom course is longer and the gates farther apart.

There are no gates in downhill racing. The goal is to go as fast as possible without falling down.

A show-off

A ski lodge

A dog team

SH

This official wore the wrong skates!

Speed skates have long blades.

Precision skating consists of solo figure skating, figure skating in pairs, and ice dancing. All involve free skating and compulsory figures. The judges award points for technique and artistic effect.

Bauble and Bangle are this year's pair-skating favorites. They are performing their freestyle routine perfectly. Their lifts and spirals come off without a tremble.

The audience is spellbound.

Poochie wants to throw them a flower when they are finished.

Annie was supposed to have made a figure eight, but this looks more like a frog.

The ice dancers Sway and Swirlynn Tandem

But here is Annie performing her freestyle routine with grace and elegance.

No one becomes a good athlete without practice, and coaches like Stan Bowser make sure that training is done properly.

Stan coaches the Bluebells icy hockey team. Here he helps Pete with his slapshot.

Workouts in the gym build strength for shooting, passing, skating, and other skills which are needed for ice hockey.

Grease, the team's physical therapist, gives Pete a massage to help his muscles relax.

Pete relaxes in other ways, too.

After the training session, members of the team shower and dress.

The Bluebells are having a tough out-of-town game with the Dog Dell Dingos. Will they win?

Coach Bowser is nervous. He's chewing four pieces of gum at a time.

Lunk Muttson has been hurt, but his only tooth seems to be all right.

Ice hockey can be dangerous, so a player wears a lot of protective clothing, including shoulder pads, elbow pads, a padded vest, knee pads, shin pads, gloves, a helmet, and pants.

This player is in the penalty box for misconduct.

Ice hockey is a fast game, and sometimes players disagree for one reason or another. Alert referees are on the ice to settle disputes quickly.

The player above wears a chin guard.

The game is over. It's a tie, and minor squabbles are forgotten. Here a Bluebell player and a Dingo player discuss the game over a cup of coffee.

Basketball is played by two five-member teams. Points are scored by tossing the ball through the opponent's basket. Since the baskets are high up, it is usually preferable to have tall basketball players on the team.

A good basketball player practices whenever he can.

The Beanpoles have a new, extra-tall defensive player. With him standing under his team's basket, their opponents, the Dogbones, are unable to score any points.

The referee checks his rule book.

In basketball the ball is moved around by dribbling, but number 3 does not seem to know that.

It's a tense moment. Members of the Dogbone team are sweating a lot, and the referee is wiping up the court so it won't be slippery.

The referees are blowing their whistles wildly.

Even radio commentator Cursel has never seen such a good defensive game.

The object of volleyball is to keep a large ball in motion from side to side over a high net by striking it with the hands before it touches the ground.

A "setter" passes the ball to a "spiker" who slams it over the net.

Water polo is played in a swimming pool. A player may touch the ball with only one hand.

Two birds bat a "birdie" in a badminton game.

Number 7 saves the ball at the last minute with a quick "dig."

Team handball is one of the fastest of all ballgames. The object is to throw a ball into the opponents' goal. A player advances the ball by throwing it from one player to another or bouncing it and may take only three steps with the ball in his hands.

Squash is played in a closed room. Players alternate hitting a ball against the front wall. The ball is supposed to be returned before it bounces on the floor twice.

Before a squash game the ball is warmed to make it bouncy.

Bowling is a popular game in which a heavy ball is rolled along a wooden alley to knock down ten wooden pins at the far end.
   But you are supposed to stay in your own alley!

A friend keeps score.

Table tennis, or Ping-Pong, is a variety of tennis played on a table, using small paddles and a lightweight hollow ball. Play can be very fast.

Pool is played on a pool table with a cue ball and fifteen balls that are driven into the pockets with a cue stick.

PREVIOUS SETS 6 4 6 0 — B. DORG — **SETS GAMES POINTS** 2 5 40

4 6 0 6 — J. MACKENPUP — 2 5 40

17.01 — HORSEY — 3.01

Linesman

In tennis, a ball is hit over a net and each player hopes that his opponent will not be able to hit it back.

This match between Mackenpup and Dorg has been very close. It is Mackenpup's turn to serve, but something has upset him.

Dorg is very calm.

Back and forth, back and forth goes the tennis ball. This spectator has gotten a sore neck from watching the fast action.

The umpire calls for play to resume.

The guests' section is filled with friends and relatives.

Netcord Judge

The ball boys pick up balls left on the court.

The players rest at the foot of the umpire's chair when they change ends of the court.

Last year's women's singles champion, Martina Navridog, is practicing her backhand.

Some male tennis stars are very popular with the young ladies.

Cricket is an Old English game. A bowler tries to bowl a ball past a batsman and get him out by hitting a wicket or "stumps."

Wicketkeeper

Wicket

Batsman

The batsman tries to knock the balls as far into the field as possible and run between the two wickets as many times as he can. The runner is out if the ball touches a wicket before he reaches it. A cricket match may last several days, with six hours' play each day.

In field hockey, two teams of eleven players each use hockey sticks to drive a small ball into each other's goal.

The batsman's partner stands at the opposite wicket and when the batsman runs, he must too. He can also be thrown out.

Bowler

Umpire

A bowler bowls six balls. After that it's another bowler's turn to bowl from the opposite wicket.

The field hockey stick has a curved blade. The left side is flat and the right side rounded. Only the flat side may be used to strike the ball.

Time for a tea break.

Golf consists of trying, with the least number of strokes, to hit a ball, with a club, from a teeing ground into a hole. There are three types of clubs: woods, irons, and putters. The first long shot from the tee to the green is made with a long-shafted, big-headed wood.

1 PAR 3 150 m

Par is the basic number of strokes needed to complete the hole.

Teeing ground

Water hazard

Most golfers ride from hole to hole in electric golf carts.

Croquet is an outdoor game played by knocking wooden balls through a series of wire wickets by means of mallets.

Pip Squeek needs a lower dart board.

A good caddie takes care of the clubs, indicates the wind direction and lay of the course, and chooses the proper clubs for the golfer.

"With this number three wood you could gently flick the ball down from the bird's nest."

Caddie cart

Caddie

Fairway

Sand trap or "bunker"

Green

Hole

A fussy golfer wearing spiked golf shoes evens up a green.

A tug-of-war

Moving the ball is not allowed!

The outfield

"Hey, get the ball to second base!"

Second base

Pitcher

First base

Mitt

In baseball, a pitcher throws a ball that a batter tries to hit. On a fair ball the batter runs to first base. If a fielder manages to throw the ball to the baseman before the runner reaches the base, the runner is out. Only one runner at a time may occupy a base. A run is scored for reaching home plate.

The teams take turns batting and fielding. Three outs and they exchange positions.

The Teddybears' star slugger, Mickey Mongrel, is up at bat.

A fast ball and *crack!* It's a long fly over the grandstands and out of the ballpark! Atta boy, Mickey! It's another homer!

A batter's helmet has an ear guard on one side.

No other pitcher put such hops and dips into his pitches as the Boomtown Batmen's pitcher. He's the terror of every other team. His pitches either go straight into the catcher's mitt, or below the batter's shoulders, or between his knees.

Bat

Catcher

Home plate

Batter's box

Home plate Umpire

TODAY:
TEDDYBEARS VS.
BOOMTOWN
BATMEN

Oops! It's dangerous to be out back of the stadium when it's Mickey's turn at bat.

HOTDOG
HAMBURGER
CHEESEBURG
CHILIBURGE
FRENCH FRIE
MILK

Husky Punter plays football on the Stumpville University team. He's a tackle. Football is a game of hard tackling and smart tactics. One team tries to carry a ball over their opponents' goal line, and the opposing side naturally tries to stop their advancing of the ball.

A marker indicates the number and position of the down.

Catkin thinks the cheerleaders are the best part of a football game.

The teams form up on the scrimmage line. Punter's team faces the Buffalo Bulldogs today. The center snaps the ball back to the quarterback and the Bulldogs charge toward Punter's team.

It's a beautiful hike.

Willy, the ballcarrier, grabs the ball and darts and dodges toward the Bulldogs' end zone. Husky Punter plows a path for him.

But watch out! Punter's shoelace has come untied.

Punter trips and in a flash the Bulldog team piles on top of Punter and Willy. It's a good thing players wear so much protective padding.

Three points are given for kicking the ball between the goal posts. Six points are given for throwing or running the ball across the goal line.

Now the Bulldogs take possession. The game continues from the line where the ball was downed. If in four downs the Bulldog team can't advance the ball ten yards, their opponents receive the ball. The players untangle themselves. But what has happened to the ball?

"There should be protective padding for the ball, too!" says Willy.

Soccer is another type of football game in which the ball is advanced only by kicking or by bouncing it off a part of the body other than the arms and hands. Only the goalkeepers may use their hands to catch, carry, or throw or stop the ball.

CUCARACHA, LEAD THE WAY! SHOW THE OTHERS HOW TO PLAY!

NORTH, SOUTH, EAST, WEST; SANTA KARAMBA IS THE BEST!

Cucaracha Island's champion team, Santa Caramba, has made it into this year's League Cup final in the Dog Dell Soccer Stadium.

A "header" is stopped at the goal.

GLUE

TAR

Santa Caramba's team members handle the ball with ease. They are not at all worried about going up against last year's champions, the Bouncers.

Everyone is in a carnival mood at the Dog Dell Stadium.

The second half draws to a close and neither team has scored a single goal.

The crowd is shocked when Puppé, the Caramba striker, collapses. But after a sip of strawberry soda, he's back on his feet.

PLAY IT, RUMBA. CARAMBA

TOMCAT FOOD

Only thirty seconds before the final whistle; a Bouncer's defender in the penalty area touches the ball with his paw. The referee indicates a penalty kick which is taken by Samba, a Santa Caramba striker. A hush settles over the crowd. *Whump!* A great kick! The goalkeeper is helpless. Santa Caramba wins 1 to 0!

The League Cup is theirs.
Photographers and hundreds of
happy fans burst onto the field.

No one seems to notice last year's champions, the defeated
Bouncers, and they are feeling very sad. It's the custom for players
to exchange shirts after a game, and Big Bruno ends up with one
that is much too small. That doesn't help cheer him up.

The coach gets a show of appreciation.

The president of Cucaracha Island accepts the congratulations of the Bouncer's hometown mayor.

After a good night's sleep even Big Bruno feels better. "After all, soccer is only a game. Sports shouldn't be taken too seriously," says Bruno. "After breakfast I think I'll go and kick the ball around. And then I'll make myself a banner from that little shirt."

Eppur si muove!

ESPAÑA 82

Grandpa Geezer and his neighbor Wheeze are old sportsmen. They don't care for jumping or running after a ball anymore. Chess is more to their liking because it is a sitting game. "That's checkmate, by the way. How about another round?"